Praises for *The Secret Sauce of Staging*

Frank J. Verni, Top Real Estate Investor / Broker / Mentor, Co-Founder – Make Money Now Investors, National Radio Show Host

I have never seen a book this comprehensive! ***The Secret Sauce of Staging*** has everything from "The Thing No One Talks About" to the "Secret Sauce of Staging."

As a real estate broker, I will be using ***The Secret Sauce of Staging*** when doing a walk-through of the home with clients. It arms them with practical, helpful tips to create the "WOW" factor. It's great information all in one place. It makes my job easier! This book is a must read!!

Anna May, Broker/Owner, Realty World Neighbors

Staging starts the moment an idea is introduced, whether visual or auditory. I knew I was dealing with a sharp professional the moment I spoke with Marlena on the phone, before I even saw her work. My confidence grew even more when I met her in person, and I saw how well put together she was herself!

Anyone can call him/herself a "stager", but Marlena has it in her bones. I highly recommend her book, ***The Secret Sauce of Staging***. As a REALTOR, I often have to moderate myself when a potential seller/ client has an extremely cluttered home. I'm delighted to have this book as a resource for clients, so I don't have to be the "bad guy" telling a potential client their place is a pig-sty.

Katy Hammond, Owner, Spruce It Up, Cleaning & Organizing

The Secret Sauce of Staging should be in the hands, and toolkit, of anyone considering the listing of their home. This incredible tool provides indispensable guidance, practical tips and complete staging success when implemented. Your home will never look better thanks to *The Secret Sauce of Staging*!

James Leis, Real Estate Investor and Mentor

The Secret Sauce of Staging is a phenomenal book full of fabulous ideas, strategies and staging secrets that make this book one of a kind! When it comes to selling property, people want more money in less time with minimum hassle. This book is your ticket. A must have!!!

Roxanne McCaslin. Realtor. New Vision Realty

I love *The Secret Sauce of Staging!* It helps you navigate through the chaos of moving. The practical tips, True Stories, Calendar, Room-by-Room Walk-Through Forms and other helpful tips are designed to help others be successful and happy in the process.

Jim T. Chong "The Wok Star" is a licensed Financial Professional, Radio Show Personality, a sought-after Master Emcee, Speaker, Community Leader, and Publicist

The Secret Sauce of Staging helps people position their homes for the market. Marlena is an exceptionally qualified individual who pays particular attention to detail and has the expertise to create a spectacular result in staging your home.

Marlena has appeared on my national Radio Show Network highlighting her expertise, but more importantly, has an incredible story behind why she does what she does.

The Secret Sauce of Staging

Getting Your Home Ready to Command Top Dollar in the Real Estate Market

Dr. Marlena E. Uhrik

Amazing-Staging
by Marlena

HOME STAGING & REDESIGN

The Secret Sauce of Staging:

Getting Your Home Ready to Command Top Dollar in the Real Estate Market

By Dr. Marlena E. Uhrik

1. BUSINESS 2. INTERIOR DECORATION
ISBN-13: 978-0-9797368-6-5

Cover design by Alicia White, Back of the Room Productions
Interior design by Kari DeCelle
Edited by Carol Quint

Printed in the United States of America

Published by
All Ways Learning, LLC
Sacramento, California
www.AllWaysLearning.org

v

Table of Contents

Acknowledgments

Special thanks to all who contributed to this book. First and foremost, my husband Bill Wheelock for his endless support, and Judy Mitchell who was the first to test drive the information in this book to help her real estate clients.

Kudos to the amazing Ray Nakamoto of Nakamoto Productions, Producer/Voice Casters, who assisted in the production of the Mindfulness MP3 that is now available on my website: amazing-staging.com/Products.

Great appreciation also goes to Katrina Sawa and Dr. Richard Greene who challenged each of us in the first place to get our book done! With their collective technical skills, knowledge and support, this book was made possible.

Thanks to all the real estate agents, brokers and investors who took the time to be interviewed and help in their own way, in order to craft this book to meet the needs of their clients.

Special gratitude also goes to friends and family who inspired and encouraged me to write, ***The Secret Sauce of Staging.*** Thank you for supporting my vision of making this book a guide for those "on the move."

It takes a village to raise a child. It takes a team to write a book!

Introduction

Who Benefits From this Book?

The Secret Sauce of Staging was created to empower people who are faced with the challenge of wanting to sell their home quickly and for top dollar. The book was also written for the person who just wants to do their own home makeover, or redesign a room. The principles and strategies discussed in this book are the same. They are just applied on a different scale, depending on what you want to do.

It is easy to feel overwhelmed when faced with a challenge, yet not know where to start. That's why I have included a section in the beginning of the book on stress management. No one talks about the stress of it all. Ideally, this book can also be used as a journal, as well as help to guide the reader into developing a plan for self-care.

As a recovering Clutter Queen, I know what it's like to take a look around at what needs to be done and then decide to go eat a chocolate chip cookie instead! It took years for me to realize that I needed to come up with something that would work for me.

As an example, I was one of those who could never find my car keys. I always thought I would be able to remember where I last put them. It never failed---there I would be running around the house, getting ready for work, and desperately searching for my keys!

I have to say, it was a revelation for me to discover that if I put my keys in the same place each time, they would be there each time. LOL.

Why Should You Read This Book?

Whether you are moving across town, around the world, or just wanting to make a change in your very own living room, this book is for you. It will give you easy tips and strategies for making the things happen with greater ease and efficiency.

You will:

- Gain greater confidence as you tackle your project
- Have tools, resources and proven strategies that will make your work easier
- Learn the "secret sauce" of staging
- Apply strategies and techniques to get that "WOW" factor in your home
- Sharpen your own abilities in analyzing the "Before and After" effects
- Improve your design acumen with an actual Case Study

What Else Will You Get Out of Reading this Book?

It is my hope that this book will provide you with the "Aha" moments that bring you new insights into a situation. Besides learning new skills, strategies and techniques for dealing with the chaos of change, it is my hope that this book provides a spiritual aspect to your journey.

I believe this process will lead to you discovering more about what things are important to you, especially when you go through the decluttering process. This all leads to having a home that you love that will nurture you and represent your fullest self-expression.

I hope this book makes you feel like you have discovered another part of you that is resilient, creative, resourceful and empowered.

What's Next?

Jump in and read this book. Give yourself fully to the Writing Opportunities. This is your book--you get to write in it! It is designed to have everything in one place, to be your guide, and to make your life easier.

Marlena has added a special hidden page on her website for those of you who have purchased this book. Go to Amazing-Staging.com/bookresources for additional FREE downloads, including forms and a MP3 Mindfulness recording she made to add to your toolkit.

Look. Love. Learn. Listen. Enjoy and have fun as you "move through" this time in your life.

"Twenty years from now you will be more disappointed by the things that you didn't do than by the ones you did do, so throw off the bowlines, sail away from safe harbor, catch the trade winds in your sails. Explore, Dream, Discover."

-Mark Twain

"Be brave enough to live creatively. The creative is the place where no one else has ever been. You have to leave the city of your comfort and go into the wilderness of your intuition. You cannot get there by bus, only by hard work, risking and by not quite knowing what you are doing. What you will discover will be wonderful: Yourself."
-Alan Alda

Chapter 1

In the Beginning

Getting your home ready to be sold on the real estate market is going to take some doing. For the most part, it is not business as usual. The current look of your home is most likely going to have to change. Even if your place already looks great, you want your home to appeal to the widest variety of potential buyers. You want to be able to provide the "secret sauce" that has people chomping at the bit to buy your home.

How to Use this Book

This interactive book is designed to reveal the "secret sauce" of home staging and support you in the process of staging your home for the real estate market.

This book does not tell you which colors to use or how to figure out design proportions. This book is designed to guide you through the principles, tips and strategies used by staging experts.

You can write in this book so that you have everything in one place. You will have a written record of things you have planned and identified that need to be done in a timely way. You will have the tools and strategies needed to make this a successful transition, while doing everything else you need to do.

Each chapter has "gold nuggets" that are the product of things learned throughout my years of staging. There are sections called "Writing Opportunity." Here you will have a chance to reflect and write down your notes, arrange your own timeline, and create your "to do" lists.

This book was also written for people who have always loved the idea of being a Home Stager, but who are not quite sure if they have what it takes.

Whether you are staging your home for the real estate market, or wanting to redesign a room or two, this book is for you. I hope this book encourages and inspires you to take that next step forward to change the things you want to change.

All of the principles of the "secret sauce" of staging, the process of planning, purging, organizing, and staging, apply to the process of not only transforming a space, but also transforming your life!

Chapter 2

What is Home Staging?

Home staging is the process of preparing a property for the real estate market so that it sells in record time and at top dollar.

It involves many factors such as planning, designing, deciding on colors and textures, procuring appropriate inventory, as well as placing furniture, accessories and artwork. Everything is all brought together to highlight the best features of the property.

Home staging involves thoughtful consideration of creating an environment that is going to connect with potential buyers.

Staging is so much more than moving furniture around to make a place look great. Staging generates the emotional experience that people experience when they walk in and say, "Wow! This is It!"

What is the Difference between Home Staging and Redesign?

Home Staging often involves bringing in new furniture and accessories to do the staging.

Redesign involves using most of the client's existing furniture and only using a few new things that will add a splash of color or "pop." A good example of this is adding new decorative pillows to an existing sofa.

"When I stand before God at the end of my life, I would hope that I would not have a single bit of talent left and could say, I used everything you gave me."

-Erma Bombeck

Chapter 3

Who are Home Stagers and What Do They Do?

Most Home Stagers I have interviewed are creative, innovative people who have some natural design skills, as well as talents for "putting things together."

Home Stagers strive to create an environment that is artistically pleasing, and at the same time, practical for everyday use.

Home Stagers, like myself, often have additional training via interior design classes, and pursue other related modalities, such as Feng Shui.

All of these elements come together to give Home Stagers their own unique look and feel to the homes they stage. Most Home Stagers love the "work" they do and do not consider it "work."

Someone who becomes a Home Stager is creative and especially loves color, design, and texture. In my opinion, being a Home Stager is like being an artist---it just happens to be that the home or property that is being staged is the huge canvas and the "artist"/ Home Stager gets to create a beautiful finished product.

A Home Stager almost automatically sees the proper placement of furniture and accessories and gets a "feeling" for what would look right in a particular place.

Even when doing a re-design (using a client's existing furniture and accessories), a Home Stager has an opportunity to transform a space into something new and exciting.

As a Home Stager, I love the act of transforming a place into something that is even more beautiful, while creating the flow within the environment. Thoughtful staging provides harmony and leads to a nurturing environment that promotes communication and "sets the stage" for people to connect.

For me, home staging expresses love, joy, beauty, and happiness and is a conduit for peace and harmony.

Writing Opportunity:

What kind of vision do you have for the space (s) you are about to create?

What's the purpose for the space?

What qualities do you want to have the space represent? (Peaceful, inviting, intriguing, etc.)

How will these qualities make you and others feel?

What will be the end result?

"You can't use up creativity. The more you use, the more you have."

-Maya Angelou

Chapter 4

But Does Home Staging Really Work?

YES!!! Staging Works!!!

- Your House Will Sell Faster: According to a survey conducted by the National Association of Realtors (NAR), the longer a property stays on the market, the lower the offers will be. Homes staged before hitting the market sell, on average, 73 percent faster than their un-staged counterparts, according to the Real Estate Staging Association.

- You Will Make More Money: A survey conducted by Coldwell Banker Real Estate Corp. discovered that staged homes are usually sold 6% above the asking price and spent less time on the market when compared to un-staged homes.

- You Will Get a Good Return on Your Investment: Another NAR survey reveals that a 1– 3% investment on home staging yields 8 –10% return, which is a good deal.

- Your Online Photos Will Stand Out: 90% of potential home buyers start their property search on the internet. Staging your home increase the visibility of your property to potential buyers.

  Source: https://goo.gl/FPe4U7

"First, have a definite, clear practical ideal; a goal, an objective. Second, have the necessary means to achieve your ends; wisdom, money, materials, and methods. Third, adjust all your means to that end."

-Aristotle

Chapter 5

Getting Ready to Get Ready: The Thing Nobody Talks About…

STRESS!!!

Before we talk about home staging, let's lay the foundation for what's ahead and make sure you are as prepared as possible for the challenge ahead.

You might be considering home staging because you're moving, because of a divorce, death in the family, downsizing, relocation, or you are just plain ready for a change.

Be prepared for an emotional rollercoaster. It's not your imagination that you might feel excited, confused, overwhelmed, and joyful all at the same time!

The mere act of moving earns a rating on the Holmes and Rahe Stress Scale as a stressful life event signaling a transition in life. Symptoms of stress can have physical, mental, social and emotional effects on the body, mind and spirit. Stress shows up as headaches, sleeplessness, rapid heart rate, anxiety, weight loss, weight gain, depression and irritability, just to name a few.

Knowing that moving can take such a toll on your health and wellbeing means you need to do your due diligence by taking care of yourself. Give yourself some time off even if it's just for a few minutes of "down time" in the midst of all the chaos.

Do your best to keep doing the self-care things that work for you such as exercising, eating well, meditating and getting plenty of rest. Just taking a few deep breaths can change how you feel emotionally, physically, mentally and spiritually. Remember to breathe!

Taking time to do at least one self-care thing a day may seem contraindicated, because it's easy to feel so overwhelmed. You might think you do not have time to take that daily 10-minute walk around the park like you usually do. Taking time for self-care pays off by creating a healthier, happier you!

In addition to taking time for yourself to insure optimum health and well-being, plan and prepare your move in advance. That is the best way to get through this stressful life event.

Take advantage of time management tools and other systems that you might already be using. Some people like the good, old-fashioned method of using paper and pencil to make a list. Others prefer using an iPad project management tracking system to plan their move. I personally like to do a "brain dump" using a yellow tablet and then apply Stephen Covey's "Four Quadrants" to help me prioritize and strategize.

"Start with the end in mind" ---a quote from Stephen Covey-- helps us see the big picture by identifying the end result, such as the move-out date. Then you can work backwards to fill in the important things that need to be done.

Be sure to calendar in your self-care so that it doesn't get left out!

Go to amazing-staging.com/bookresources and get your FREE Calendar to help you plot out your move.

Writing Opportunity:

What are some things that you enjoy doing that help you get through the day?

Read a book? Listen to music? Have lunch with a friend? Take a walk?

List 3-5 ways you will take care of yourself during this stressful transition time:

1.

2.

3.

4.

5.

"There is nothing in a caterpillar that tells you it's going to be a butterfly."
-Buckminster Fuller

Chapter 6

We're Almost There---Setting the Stage to Stage---First Things First

From a Home Stager's point of view, the most important thing you can do to get ready to stage is:

Purge. Purge. Purge.

Start the purging process by identifying one small area that needs to be cleaned, sorted out and organized. It's recommended to start small and experience the accomplishment and satisfaction of getting rid of things that you no longer need or use. It's amazing how things like clutter can sneak up on you. Before you know it you can't open up a kitchen drawer because of all the stuff in it.

While you are planning, organizing, purging, and packing, remember to sort things into categories. Sort things that you are definitely going to toss, things you are going to donate, things that need to be repaired, and things you love and want to take with you.

Once you start out and complete something, like the kitchen "junk drawer", you can advance to something more complicated, like a kitchen cabinet, pantry, or closet.

True Story: I remember when I was getting ready to move and decided to start the purging process by going through my kitchen cabinet where I had stored paper bags, an assortment of glass jars, thermoses and water bottles. Imagine my surprise as I started to uncover 15 brand new water bottles that I had acquired at various health fairs, business conferences, and other special events. I had conveniently stored and forgotten about them! Guess where those 15 brand new water bottles wound up? A donation to charity--- along with a multitude of other things that I discovered I had never used!

Writing Opportunity:

What is the first area you will purge?

What will be your goal?

Getting rid of duplicates? Which ones?

Organizing things into categories? Which categories?

How will you feel once this part is done?

"When I was 5 years old, my
 mother always told me
that happiness was the key to
 life. When I went to
school, they asked me what I
wanted to be when I
grew up. I wrote down
'happy'. They told me I didn't
understand the assignment, and
I told them they didn't
understand life."
-John Lennon

Chapter 7

Everyone Gets in on the Act: All Hands-on Deck for a Family Meeting

During this process, it is also critical to include the members of your family, so that you have "buy-in" and everyone is on the same page. Remember, everyone (age-appropriate) can be part of this process---even the purging!

- Have a Family Meeting to talk about the move and what it means to each member of your family.
- Listen to what other family members say. This can be an emotional time for the children, too. Be sure to address feelings about what the move means to the kids, as they may also have concerns.
- Discuss ideas and listen for solutions
- Decide on who is going to do what, and when that is going to happen.
- Post charts, calendar or timeline, so everyone can see the "big picture" and be part of the team effort

- Be somewhat flexible with goals. Keep moving forward, even though everything might not get done according to the exact timeline
- Kids can purge their stuff, too, like toys, books and clothes. Remember, what they don't want can be donated to charities.
- Set up a reward system for yourself and others. For example, kids get proceeds from the sale of their items at your family garage sale, etc.
- Show pictures of the new digs, whether you have pictures on your cellphone, pamphlets or flyers of the new place, or from part of your on-line search.
- Take family members to see their new digs. If possible, consider letting them choose their own bedrooms.
- Let the kids dream with you about the new home and imagine all the fun activities you will be doing there.
- If kids are going to a new school, it is helpful to make arrangements to introduce them to their new teacher and classmates, see their classroom, playground, and cafeteria.

Writing Opportunity:

Take a look at your calendar.

When will you schedule your family meeting?

Who will do what?

What new ideas did family members have?

How will you implement your ideas and work together?

"Gratitude is the healthiest of all human emotions. The more you express gratitude for what you have, the more likely you will have even more to express gratitude for."

-Zig Ziglar

Chapter 8

The Secret Sauce of Staging: Let the Magic Begin!

The Top 5 Things You Should Know about Staging Your Home for the Real Estate Market.

Think about each one of these 5 things and how they apply to you and your current situation. This becomes your "To Do" List. Insert them into your calendar.

1. **Appeal to the largest number of potential buyers, so that your property sells quickly and for the highest price possible.**

   - It's critical that if you want to get top dollar, your place will have to shine and be sparkly clean.

   - Make sure that you create a feeling of openness and spaciousness by removing clutter and excess furniture.

   - It is recommended to keep everything as neutral as possible especially interior paint, carpet and tile.

Dr. Marlena E. Uhrik

Writing Opportunity:

What can you do to make sure your property will appeal to the highest number of potential buyers?

What things need to be cleaned?

When will you schedule the cleaning portion of this process?

What excess furniture will you remove?

Does anything need to be painted? If so, which neutral color will you choose?

2. Emphasize your home's best features.

- Think about what you loved about your home when you first saw it. Was it the bay window in the kitchen? Open arches throughout the house? The long entryway? The fireplace in the living room? The view from the backyard?

- Could some of these features be highlighted with plants, artwork, floral arrangements, special lighting, or other accessories?

- Even with emphasizing your home's best features, remember to use the KISS approach---Keep It Simple Sweetheart.

Writing Opportunity:

What are your home's best features?

How can you emphasize them?

What items will you use to emphasize your home's best features?

How will these items enhance the look of your home's best features?

How can you use the KISS approach? (Hint—Less is better.)

3. Provide "move-in" condition whenever possible.

- Most people want their new home to be in pristine condition when they move in. People are so busy with their lives that they do not want to clean a dirty oven, paint three bedrooms, repair holes in the wall, or replace carpet before they move into their new home.

- Of course, having "move in" condition, does not apply if the buyers are real estate investors who are going to do a fix and flip, or someone who is handy and can perhaps negotiate a lower price for moving into a place "as is."

- When you think about "move-in" condition think about the condition of both the exterior and interior of your property.

Writing Opportunity:

What can you do to have the "move-in" ready condition for your home?

Would you be willing to negotiate a lower price if your home is not in "move-in condition"?

What is the condition of the exterior of your property?

What is the condition of the interior of your property?

What still needs to be done? Calendar these things into your schedule.

4. Declutter.

- Decluttering is the "secret sauce" of making things look clean, open, and inviting. That's why it's important to declutter your home in preparation for the real estate market. Make sure you have plenty of openness and spaciousness in each and every room.

- Decluttering makes it easier for the potential buyer to visualize themselves living in your home. It's recommended to start the decluttering on a small scale, like a drawer or closet, and work up to something big, like an entire room. Congratulate yourself on small victories!

- By removing personal items such as photos, tokens, souvenirs, excessive amounts of books, magazines, stacks of paper on a desk, clutter on the kitchen counters and other surfaces, you can achieve an inspiring visual effect.

- Some stagers recommend removing religious artifacts so as to appeal to the largest number of potential buyers.

Writing Opportunity:

Where will you start to declutter?

What kind of supplies, like storage containers and trash bags, will you need to complete this project?

What is the end result you have in mind?

What will that end result bring you?

How will you feel when you have accomplished your goal?

5. **Create the emotional connection that potential buyers feel when they walk into your home and say "This is IT."**

   - Many people experience their home as their sanctuary---a safe place to rest, relax, and to feel loved and nurtured.

   - To make the look and feel of the home appealing, use items that bring physical and emotional comfort. These can be things like throwing a blanket over a chair, or putting pillows on the sofa, flowers in a vase, books and a candle on the coffee table, a touch of greenery here and there, and a bowl of fruit on the kitchen counter.

   - Finding ways to appeal to the senses will help bring the balance and harmony that many people crave and strive for, especially if they have had a long, hard day at work, or are going through a difficult time, or just want to feel "at home." Prospective buyers will be able to imagine themselves in your beautifully staged home.

Writing Opportunity:

Is your home your sanctuary?

What nurtures you?

What makes you feel "at home?"

List ways you can appeal to the senses and create that emotional connection when people see your home.

How will prospective buyers feel when they are in your home?

Chapter 9

What You Need to Know to Create that WOW Factor!

The 5 Easy and Affordable Projects that Help Promote that WOW Factor and What We Did That Sold Our Condo on the First Day

As a Home Stager, I was really excited to stage one of our own properties that we recently sold. My husband and I had purchased a condo when we first moved to Sacramento years ago. We really loved the condo and lived in it for 10 years until we decided to move into something bigger and rent out our condo.

After renting the condo out for 5 years, we decided we wanted to upgrade it and put it on the "smoking hot" real estate market here in Sacramento. We got 3 offers on the first day of our Open House. Of course, we went with the highest bidder which was $12,000 over the original asking price!

Here are 5 things we did that created the WOW factor and got us top dollar:

1. Focused on first impressions! That meant the garage door, too!!! We made sure, our garage door was in good working condition, and the trim around the garage door and exterior windows looked fresh. We swept away dirt and cobwebs that had collected around the windows and on the porch.

2. Spruced up curb appeal. We trimmed outside shrubs, pulled weeds, and added new tanbark. We repaired the security screen door, spray painted it, updated the front door with a fresh coat of paint and added

bright, new shiny hardware. We also bought a new door mat just to make sure everything looked new and spiffy.

3. Painted the interior walls a neutral color. We used a neutral color to help people connect with the physical surroundings, so they could picture their furnishings in our place. Fortunately, we did not have any black, orange or red walls. This can be a show stopper for many people who cannot see beyond the intense colors. We considered painting an accent wall with a trending color, but ran out of time and motivation.

4. Updated kitchen cabinets with paint and new hardware. Putting a fresh coat of paint on the old, tired-looking cabinets was an easy and inexpensive thing to do. Plus, adding modern kitchen hardware really upped the look and feel of the kitchen.

5. Re-caulked the kitchen sink and bathroom sink(s) and area around the toilets. The existing caulking was at least 10 years old and by applying a thin, new coat of caulking material, we brightened up the appearance that added to a new, fresh look and feel.

Of course, the condo was beautifully staged, and by emphasizing the architectural features of the property, it was easy to create that emotional "Wow" effect. For more details and videos of the process, see my website: amazing-staging.com and click on Videos---A Day in the Life of a Home Stager.

There are many other things that can be done to prepare your home for the real estate market. Many people update bathroom fixtures, light fixtures and countertops. The extent of preparation depends on your budget, timeline and intention.

Some people just want to sell their home "as is." They do not want to put time and money into getting their property ready for "move-in condition." Everybody's circumstances are different. It's just important to know that chances are good that you will be getting less money, maybe even fewer offers, if you do not update/upgrade your home for the real estate market.

Writing Opportunity:

What is your plan for creating your own WOW Factor?

Chapter 10

Before and After Pictures

Master Bedroom

This spacious Master Bedroom was dull and uninspiring and with limited appeal. It was "decorated" in all brown with mismatched lamps, white Venetian blinds, and no artwork on the walls. Clients still wanted brown tones, so Marlena brought in a comforter that had a beautiful robin-egg blue color with a brown border, and matching pillows and drapes. Beautifully framed photographs of the couple, candles, elegant lamps and artwork created a peaceful, lush, romantic setting.

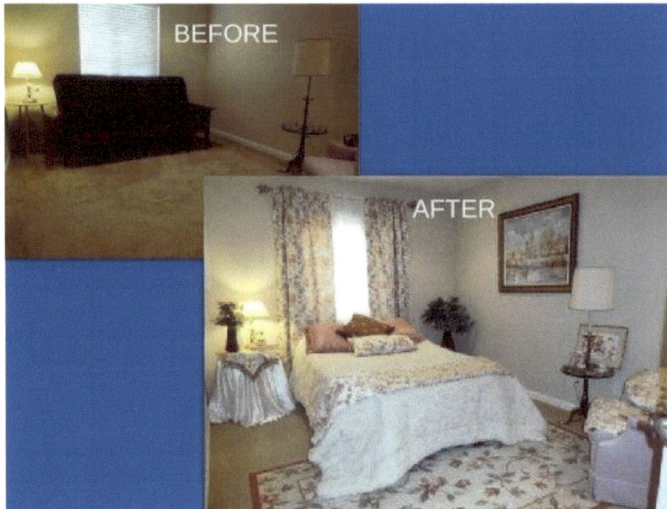

A "Whatever" Room

This downstairs guest bedroom was not well-defined or developed by the homeowners. It became a "catch-all" room with mismatched furniture. After my consultation with the clients, they agreed that they did not have the time or the imagination to "fix it up." They decided that they wanted to create a luxurious guest bedroom that could ultimately be used as an Airbnb. A complete transformation occurred with rich brocade drapes, pillows, a rug, artwork and accessories.

Case Study: What's wrong here?

List 10 things you would change.

1.

2.

3.

4.

5.

6.

7.

8.

9.

10.

The Finished Product

Here are some of some of the things that were done to stage this space:

1. Removed clutter from the desk
2. Removed clutter from the shelves
3. Organized things on shelves
4. Put things in matching containers
5. Got rid of one monitor
6. Added a lamp for extra lighting
7. Added a bamboo plant for something green
8. Added a rug
9. Added a chair with pillows
10. Added a trash can in corner

Writing Opportunity:

What was your experience of seeing the difference in the "Before and After" pictures of this setting?

How will this experience help you in developing your "Before and After" look?

What did you learn by doing the Case Study?

How will you use what you learned by doing the Case Study?

What results will that bring?

"The way to get started is to quit talking and begin doing."

-Walt Disney

Chapter 11

The 5 Last Minute Things You Can Do Before Every Showing---Kids Can Help, Too!

The "heat is on" when it comes to living in your home while you are trying to sell it. You must be prepared for potential buyers to come through at any time to check it out. This means having your home ready at all times.

 Potential buyers want to visualize themselves living in each home they see, trying to decide if it's a "fit." Fortunately, most real estate agents who show your home will work with you and your schedule to help minimize the stress of just "dropping by."

Here are 5 Last Minute Things You Can Do Before Every Showing---Kids can help, too!!!

1. Stand outside of your house and do a quick visual check-in. Are there flyers or newspapers on the front porch? Is the lawn freshly mowed? Is the porch swept? Are there cobwebs or dirt on the window sills?

2. Freshen the air inside. Is there a lingering smell from the fish or broccoli you cooked last night for dinner? Be sensitive to that first-smell-impression. Many people remember smells associated with events, so make sure, your home smells good! Be careful not to overdo it with strong sprays/scents/perfumes as many people are allergic to the chemicals in these products. Using aromatherapy and environmentally-safe cleaning products can give you the results you want by providing a

pleasant sensory experience for potential buyers.

3. Speed clean. Focus on the kitchen and bathrooms. This can be done practically in the blink of an eye. A quick rub with a damp paper towel or washcloth can get the water spots, hairs and toothpaste out of the sink and have things looking spiffy. Make sure you put the toilet seat and lid down. It's good Feng Shui and just looks better.

4. Take out the trash---a simple and easy thing to do. It's the little things that can make a big difference. This could be a quick and easy thing for a kid to do, too.

5. Vacuum the carpet. If you only have a few minutes to get this task done, focus on the room that people will see first, such as the living room.

P.S. Keep the lights on (LEDs, of course), and window coverings adjusted to let lots of light into the space.

Bonus---Create a junk drawer for the "Big Sweep" or use a laundry basket for the Big, Big Sweep! I love this technique and I have used it myself lots of the time.

True Story: As a recovering clutter queen, I have to share that I have had to resort to some Big Time "Sweep" strategies.

The Secret Sauce of Staging

Many years ago, shortly after I had gotten married to my former husband, our parents announced that they wanted to come and visit us in our new apartment.

We procrastinated getting ready for the visit until the actual day was upon us. We wound up "sweeping" everything that was loose and on the floor into the bathtub (everything from dirty socks, dirty dishes, old magazines, etc.) Then we pulled the shower curtain closed!

There I was hoping no one would dare pull that shower curtain back, exposing a huge array of stuff that got crammed and placed "behind the scenes"! I'll never know if anyone actually pulled that shower curtain back to take a peek out of curiosity. Perhaps I might have been a bit naïve to think no one would peek behind the curtain?

P.S. Be sure to have an opaque shower curtain! LOL.

Writing Opportunity:

What did you discover when you looked outside your house at the curb appeal?

How will you freshen up the air inside your home?

Who will do the speed cleaning?

Who will take out the trash?

How will you have your home ready for a showing at any time?

Chapter 12

Did I Do It Right?

Staging is such a personal experience. Staging is like the artist's canvas and every artist/stager interprets things in a different way.

Get inspired! Let staging be part of your self-expression. Here are some ideas to grow your staging confidence.

- Get ideas by talking to friends
- Go to Open House events to see how homes are staged and what's trending
- Look in magazines for ideas
- Use your own creative genius
- Hire a professional Home Stager
- Talk to your Real Estate Agent to get feedback
- Use apps that are available on your cellphone
- Look at Pinterest for ideas

Happiness at Last/An Opportunity for Reflection

Congratulate yourself, whether you chose this book to help you get your home ready for the real estate market, or you wanted to learn more about re-designing a room, or staging your entire home. You have begun a journey!

As many people have said, it's the journey that counts. How was this journey? Did you hit some bumps in the road? Did things go as smoothly as you thought they would?

What were some of the things you learned about yourself through this process? What worked? What didn't work as well as you thought it would?

I hope *The Secret Sauce of Staging* has given you an opportunity to learn something new about yourself and others and the things that are important to you. As with any change, there are opportunities for learning and opportunities for growth.

Review your Writing Opportunities so that you can look back on this experience and acknowledge yourself and others for being part of this process.

Thank you for allowing *The Secret Sauce of Staging* to be part of your "moving" journey.

ACTION STEP

Decide what might be the next steps for you in this personal journey of discovery. Keep finding new ways to learn and grow.

What's next for you? What are your new goals?

Help yourself get out of the comfort zone and explore new things and new ways of being. Keep things positive and always look for the lesson learned.

Whether you live near or far, (thanks to modern technology) here are some additional ways that I can help you and others:

Provide **FREE** Consultation, Help You Create the WOW Factor, Declutter, Organize, Stage Your Property, Re-purpose a Room, Re-design Your Living Environment, Seasonal Decorating, Table Setting and more.

All of these services, techniques, and strategies can be applied in many different arenas including: Glamping, Airbnb, Bed and Breakfast, Vacation Rentals, Fix and Flips, and Short/Long Rentals to Traveling Professionals and more.

Marlena has added a special hidden page on her website for those of you who have purchased this book. Go to Amazing-Staging.com/bookresources for additional free downloads.

Continue your journey! Contact me **TODAY** for your **FREE** Consult and let the journey continue! Go to my website: amazing-staging.com. Let's start **TODAY**!

"Only when we are brave enough to explore the darkness will we discover the infinite power of our light."

-Brene' Brown

Check Lists and Forms

Go to:

Amazing-Staging.com/bookresources

for downloadable Check Lists, Forms and

other **FREE** materials for people who

have purchased this book.

Room-by-Room Checklist---What all Rooms Need

Make sure you do these things:

- ✓ Declutter
- ✓ Clean
- ✓ Organize
- ✓ Repair
- ✓ Create a Focal Point
- ✓ Identify furniture, artwork and other artifacts to be removed
- ✓ Evaluate window coverings/light fixtures/hardware
- ✓ Decide to paint or not

Use the following page to start to create a room-by-room checklist so that you feel you have covered everything. Write out your plan for each room/area on a separate sheet. This becomes your "To Do" list. Additional "To Do" lists are available at my website: amazing-staging.com/bookresources

Each property will vary according to the location, number of rooms, types of rooms, how rooms are used, and outdoor space---including front, back, and side yards, too.

Identify the purpose of each room and be thoughtful about how you would stage this room highlighting or creating a focal point or best feature.

For instance, the focal point (a main feature in a room) could be the bed in a bedroom. On the other hand, some bedrooms get converted to office space so the desk would most likely be the focal point.

Refer to your calendar and your To Do List to make sure all areas of planning are covered.

The Secret Sauce of Staging

Use sections of this guidebook to review the details that take you from purging, organizing, cleaning, moving and staging.

Be prepared to multi-task: decluttering and packing at the same time and for more than one family member. In addition, you will be working on everything else you need to do! That's another reason why having a stress management plan is going to be critical! Lots going on...

Dr. Marlena E. Uhrik

Doing the Walk Through "To Do List"

Name of Room _____

Purpose of Room _____

What supplies/materials do you need to stage this room?

Before:

Declutter---What areas need to be decluttered?

Clean---What things need to be cleaned?

During:

Focal point---What will you create as a focal point in this room?

After:

What needs to be done?

Notes:

Showtime! Open House. Don't Leave Anything Out!

Remember to:

- ☐ Make everything sparkly clean!
- ☐ Declutter all countertops, especially in the kitchen and bathrooms.
- ☐ Create that focal point in the rooms that you are staging (not all rooms need to be staged.)

Listed here are the things already mentioned in this book and some other staging hacks that work:

- ☐ Curb Appeal: trim lawn, shrubs, trees, weeds
- ☐ Area outside the front of the house---clean off dirt on garage door, window sills, and front porch. Add plants with a "pop" of color
- ☐ Entryway: keep free of clutter
- ☐ Bathrooms: hang fresh towels. Get new ones that are extra fluffy for the Open House. Remove things like toothbrushes, toothpaste, deodorant, etc.
  Make it feel spa-like!!!
- ☐ Living Room: remember KISS (Keep It Simple Sweetheart). Less is more. Create that emotional connection. If needed, add a "pop" of color with new toss pillows on the sofa/chairs.
- ☐ Dining Room: Place centerpiece in the middle of the table. Add a table runner or placemats. Cloth napkins give it a touch of elegance. "Stage" the table by adding place settings.
- ☐ Kitchen: Remove things from the countertop, including small appliances, such as toasters and

mixers, dishes, and pots and pans. Add fresh dish towels.

☐ Bedrooms: Do what your Mother told you to do---LOL: Make the bed. Pick up your clothes. Put your things away. Clear off the top of your dresser. Open the windows to let the room "air out."

☐ Closets: Clean them out! This includes clothes closets, linen closets, and pantries. People want to imagine how their things are going to fit into those spaces. The less stuff you have in there, the bigger the space will appear.

☐ Laundry Room: Even millennials are reported to like laundry rooms! Keep your space organized, clean and free of debris and spilled detergent.

Amazing Staging

Certificate

I did an

Amazing Staging

job!

Name_____

Date Started_____

Date Completed_____

Appendix

For a FREE MP3 download of a Mindfulness exercise, go to: amazing-staging.com/bookresources

For a Calendar to help you plot out your move, and extra copies of Room-By-Room To Do List, go to: amazing-staging. com/bookresources

For more details and videos, go to:

amazing-staging.com/Videos---A Day in the Life of a Home Stager.

About the Author

Dr. Marlena E. Uhrik, CEO

Amazing Staging by Marlena

Marlena's career path has taken her through a very full and extensive journey. Even as a child, Marlena always wanted to be a teacher. As a life-long learner, Marlena became an educator and went on to get her Doctorate degree in Educational Leadership.

For 15 years, Marlena served as the Executive Director of a non-profit organization she started called, The Kids' Breakfast Club (TKBC). She created TKBC to help feed hungry kids and provide educational activities for them when school was not in session. TKBC continues to serve children and their families and will be celebrating its 25th Anniversary!

She has won numerous local, state, and national awards and recognition for the work that she has done. Some of her proudest moments include being nominated as a Community Hero and running as a 1996 Olympic Torchbearer.

She was also recognized in the United States Congressional Record for her contribution to children and their families. Marlena has had a private practice as a holistic health educator, became an award-winning author, a voice over artist, national conference presenter, and now, a real estate investor and Home Stager.

Recently "retired" as a Consultant for the California Department of Education, Marlena has taken her love for staging and has become a professional Home Stager. "I feel like I have this opportunity to do something I have always loved doing-Staging! To me, it's not work."

Marlena says she has been staging homes since she was four years old! It all began with her favorite dollhouse as a child. Even then, she loved the creative process of moving things around to have that transformational "aha" effect.

Looking back, she realizes that she has been staging everything from classrooms, schools, offices, as well as the homes she and her husband purchased, fixed, and sold for a huge profit.

Over the years, Marlena has sharpened her natural talents by taking a variety of interior design classes, including Feng Shui, to expand her knowledge and expertise.

She has professionally staged homes in the Sacramento region for the last 10 years, and she is especially sought after by real estate agents, brokers and real estate investors.

www.ingramcontent.com/pod-product-compliance
Lightning Source LLC
Chambersburg PA
CBHW041530090426

42738CB00035B/20